THE FIREHORSES OF SAN FRANCISCO

THE FIREHORSES
OF SAN FRANCISCO

By NATLEE KENOYER

WESTERNLORE PRESS . . . 1970 . . . LOS ANGELES 90041

Library of Congress Catalog Card No. 75-110157

PRINTED IN THE UNITED STATES OF AMERICA BY WESTERNLORE PRESS

To CAROLYN
who is always encouraging

Introduction

ANY BOOK OF HISTORY must have the help of many to make it authentic and interesting. This book was fashioned with loving memories because I wanted everyone to remember those great horses of the Fire Service. By the same token, those who contributed the facts found herein, I am sure, did so for much the same reason.

Every fireman I contacted answered with many suggestions of where to find what I was seeking. One retired Captain sent me his daughter's scrapbook, wherein I found a wealth of personal stories of the horses. The files of the San Francisco *Chronicle* gave me leads to the discovering of more facts.

The San Francisco Fire Museum loaned us the use of many action pictures. Mr. Chet Born, Inspector, Photo Unit, San Francisco Fire Department, was especially helpful in copying many of the rare photos found in the Museum. Faithful reproductions of equipment can be credited to the Museum and to this generous assistance.

The Wells Fargo History Room added their contribution of the pictures that go to enrich this book and make it pictorially complete.

To all these gracious people and institutions I give my sincere thanks. Through the help of such friends, may the memory of San Francisco's firehorses live forever on!

NATLEE KENOYER.

Contents

Illustrations

Foreword

IN SETTING DOWN all the information in this book for public consideration, my purpose is to present to those so far removed from the horse and buggy days, a picture of an era that brought out the best in horses. To prove, perhaps, that these beautiful animals are something more than dumb brutes. The author lived through this era, and the memories are still bright and clear of the excitement of the fire service, brightened mainly by the sight of the horses, themselves, galloping down the street pulling the smoking steam pumper. Three massive, white horses; their ears back; the pink showing in their flared nostrils; a sight one can never forget.

There are few drivers alive today who can give an accurate accounting of the lives and actions of the fire-horses, and it took some doing to find and interview these men who were responsible for the training and care of the courageous animals. Those who truly loved their horses are the ones who can account for the many personal stories I have repeated in this book. Their recollections are priceless.

I present this book with the hope that its pages will influence the reader to love and respect the firehorses, as did the author. What I have told is all true.

NATLEE KENOYER.

THE FIREHORSES OF SAN FRANCISCO

The Beginning

IT WAS DURING an epidemic of cholera that horses were first used to fight a fire. The year was 1832. The working force of the New York City fire department was weakened by sickness and death. Not enough men could be mustered to draw the hand engines to a fire. Something drastic had to be done. And it was this emergency that brought the horse into use. The new method gave the department something to think about. Suddenly they became aware of the increase of speed and efficiency; the ability to move more equipment. It was indeed something to ponder. The word spread throughout the country that horses might be the answer to the fire problem. San Francisco, in light of their own difficulty, thought much about it. However, it was not until some years later that horses were put to actual use.

Before the advent of motorized equipment, men handled the fire carts by their own strength. Chiefly, they were two-wheeled affairs, light weight and easily moved, but lacking in maximum efficiency. However, there must have been some foresight, because the first steam engine ever built—in London, England in 1829—was, because of its great weight, constructed so it could be drawn by horses. This, perhaps, was the first indication that horses would and could be used.

It took the cholera epidemic of 1832 to prove that fire equipment could be successfully drawn by horses and would most assuredly add to the speed of getting to a fire. But it was not until 1863 that firehorses began to be installed as a permanent part of the department. On this date a newly designed steam engine was received by the Pennsylvania Engine Company No. 12 of San Francisco.

Even though some companies continued to draw their engines by hand, the method was on the wane. It was on an evening in August of that some year that three black horses, known as a spike team, were harnessed to the new steam wagon and trotted through the streets. A route was covered as a test. And the combination of team and equipment convinced the department that this was possibly the answer.

The first alarm ever responded to by a horse-drawn apparatus was on October 14, 1863. It was a still alarm, which means no box was pulled or no particular warning was sounded, but it was actually the first real call for the firehorses. And it was the Pennsylvania Company and their new steam engine. The smoking steamer was a dramatic sensation as it sped to a fire in a box factory near Fremont and Market Streets—to definitely prove that larger equipment could certainly be moved with greater speed and efficiency.

By a strange coincidence, Pennsylvania Company was not only pioneer with the horse-drawn equipment, but was the first company to be given a number. During the reorganization of 1866 it became known as Company No. 6. At the August 19, 1863 fire the Pennsylvania Company responded with its three black horses, and, on August 21, 1921, the San Francisco Company No. 6 responded to the last fire in which horses were used. Again, the engine was drawn by three black horses.

No tongue or pen will ever be able to pay a fitting tribute to the noble animal that was such an important part of San Francisco's fire service. It is true, that down through the ages, the horse has been the most faithful servant and companion of mankind. Not only does San Francisco, but everyone in the world of fire fighting, owes a debt of gratitude to these four-footed athletes.

20

There are many sentimental stories, fond memories, touched with the practicability of purpose and accomplishment, about the horses who gave all they had that the city might be secure from flames. The idea of horses used for fire fighting in San Francisco was something of an undertaking in itself because of the geography of the city. It was admittedly a challenge with its many great hills. Unusually steep grades made the dragging of heavy loads by horses a real task. It was a challenging undertaking to organize a fire service that would cover such a city. There were many things to think about, and many problems to work out.

In the beginning each fireman furnished his own horses for the wagon he drove. He fed and cared for them out of the salary he received. However, this served to bring forth its own pride of accomplishment. Each fireman tried to have the most efficient unit in the firehouse.

One fireman told of a horse he owned, a blue roan of undetermined breeding, but a fiery animal. The rest of the firemen could never figure out how Frank got to the scene of a fire so quickly. Having time on his hands Frank figured out a hanger for harness, an overhead rigging connected with a small bell in his house. On the first tap the light came on, the door opened and by the time he got to the stable the horse was waiting for him to drop the harness on him. This man's ingenuity later established a pattern worked out by others that revolutionized the whole harnessing process. The biggest problem of the time was to find men willing to fight fires at almost impossible odds. It took brave men and good horses, but most of all it took water.

In the early days of 1849 water was scarce in San Francisco. There were a few wells scattered around the city, but most of the water came from cisterns. The first water supply was simply a one-horse cart with two kegs. This certainly couldn't be counted on for fire fighting. The first water supply for the San Francisco Fire Department was developed in 1850 when J. P. Baker and Samuel Crocker were permitted to sink a cistern in Pine Street, near Sansome. Running a pipe underground, they brought the termination point near the firehouse. At this end was a pump. This began, for a while, to be the pattern of fire fighting. But again, it limited the area

to be served, and more cisterns were constructed, at strategic points throughout the city where wells were not
available. Here was where the steam pumper came into
active use and was the most important piece of equipment in any firehouse—and, no doubt, the best remembered.

At first the pumper was drawn by two horses. It was
built in Pennsylvania and was called the Selby Steamer.
The second important piece, of course, was the two-
wheeled hose cart, drawn by one horse. Every firehouse
was not dependent on horses and many times, when
speed was essential, some expressman's horse might be
pressed into service. Indeed there was much to be de-
sired. Precious time was lost during these emergencies,
and the loss of property was great. And along with this
lack of efficiency, there was little evidence of warning.

*An old print of one of the
most interesting apparatus
in the New York Fire De-
partment, in 1884. It was a
portable water tank. Hose
lines, from a fireboat, were
used to fill the vehicle.*

—New York Fire College Library.

22

For a long while there was no gong in the firehouse. The firemen had to count the blasts of the whistle on the water works tower, after someone had given the warning. The animals used in the horse-manned companies wore their harness day and night, and, in the desperate effort for readiness, it was only removed for grooming. Eventually provision was made for a watchman, on duty in the city hall tower, who would strike a bill bell by means of a mechanical lever. The other fire bells throughout the city would then join in the alarm.

From the watchman's station in the city hall tower, a signal was hung during the day—pointing in the direction of the fire. After dark, a night light, such as a lantern, was used. It is a far cry from those days of struggle for a more efficient service, to the elaborate alarm system of today—but everything must have a beginning. The crawl comes before the walk. Great need suggested

Hand drawn fire wagon—Crescent Company No. 10, San Francisco Fire Dept.

—Courtesy, History Room, Wells Fargo Bank.

and forced the changes. Cisterns could be built, wells could be dug, equipment could be designed for every use, brave men could be found to offer their services to fight any conflagration that threatened lives, homes and livelihoods—but to find animals to withstand the rigors of fire fighting was the biggest problem of all. One thing called for another.

The first firemen were trained by experience. The first horses were trained by trial and error. However, as more companies began to use horses it posed another problem. With the introduction of horses there came the need for stables. Then the need for more horses, and the greater need for replacements of animals and equipment. But the coming of the horse brought the biggest changes of all.

With the passage of a law authorizing the paid department of 1866, horses came into general use in every firehouse, and the buildings were refitted to take care of the new order of things. The firehorse was forced to meet any challenge offered by man's invention. Until firehouses were established into districts, the terrain at first was difficult, the distances great. However, weight meant nothing to the firehorse, no wagon was too heavy to pull.

In the day of their need, the firehorses were numbered in the many hundreds. In a city like San Francisco, with its many districts, hundreds of wagons were required which, in turn, demanded almost a thousand horses. All this served to make a history unequalled anywhere in the world.

There are countless stories about the fire service, not only of San Francisco, but all over the United States. A letter to the present Fire College in New York City will answer almost any question about the history of the various departments, even about the fire caused by Mrs. O'Leary's cow which brought equipment from New York City by flat car to help fight the famous Chicago fire. But because of its terrain, San Francisco probably offers the most colorful history of all. This hilly city, with its many challenges, leads the nation in its fight against fire.

There are few people today who can remember the fire signal sounding, and the rush to the curbing to watch these courageous firehorses give all they had so a city might be safe from flames. No horse history can boast of more excitement or daring—not even the crusades, or the races of the Roman chariots—and certainly none with so solemn a purpose.

The "speed" harness, as finally evolved. Note bottom-snap collars, and "troica" formation of the typical three-horse team.

—Courtesy, History Room, Wells Fargo Bank.

Equipment, horses and men pose in front of one of San Francisco's very early fire-houses.

—Courtesy, San Francisco Fire Museum.

The Breeding of Firehorses

WHEN THE FIRST CALLS went out for firehorses the request called for big, powerful and swift animals. Each time the department located a horse that apparently filled the primary requirements, he was hitched up with a trained horse to an engine of great weight and given a strong, heavy pull up one of the city's seven hills. If the animal stood up under this test, he was then turned over, still hot and panting, to the veterinary surgeon of the department. Then he was given an inch-by-inch examination from muzzle to tail. His lungs were tested. His muscle tension was noted, his legs were examined. Then, if still found to be satisfactory, the animal was put to work for a month, on trial.

During the month he was watched closely for his ability and adaptability. Was he easy to train, of good speed, quick in action, showing no disposition to stumble, and could he back properly? All these attributes were important. Nothing could be left to chance in the need for emergency. If he proved adept in all these requirements he was purchased. The average price was around $300.00. But even this method had its drawbacks. There were not enough of these horses.

At first, buying any horse that seemed fit and had most of these requirements appeared to be the answer, but then the decision was made to have a special horse for the department. This proved a slow method, because breeding requirements began to be noted. The right weight, the best size and endurance were a must. But, finally, the department had forty-seven fine animals in its use.

However, in May of 1873, an epidemic known commonly as "equine influenza" attacked the forty-seven horses. In its malignant form, death usually came in seven days. So rapid was the spread of the disease that in less than one week all the horses of the department were more or less affected, and many died. An appeal was made to all public institutions, under control of the city, as well as private firms owning large, heavy horses. All were asked to hold in readiness, all spare animals. But owing to the presence of the disease among the private horses also, it was impossible to replace the animals of the department that had died.

Some of the fire apparatus was entirely without horses. Ropes were attached, and volunteers called upon to stand by to pull the engines. But, fortunately, no serious fires broke out during this crisis. However, during a few trial runs, where the men had to experience the awkwardness and futile strength in handling these wagons, it served to remind the department and the public how important their firehorses were to the city's safety. Then started the job of replacing the horses and putting the department back on its feet. The need was for an animal weighing between 1300 and 1400 pounds; actually too large for carriage use, and too small for draft use. But, now, the department knew the type horse it wanted and needed.

It took much time to replace the animals lost in the epidemic, and as the department was constantly growing the demand for suitable stock was constant. But even with this wide search for the right animal, several hundred of the finest horses of their kind in the world were finally incorporated into the department. Never again would there be doubt of the quality of replacements. Come what may, every firehorse would be supplied, even to districts newly assigned.

The chosen animal was a magnificent horse—great and wide-chested, with tight skin—compact, with solid muscles, well-proportioned limbs — full of life and strength. This horse was noble, and San Francisco could well be proud of it. Such was the ideal animal for the service, and this is what they sought.

It soon became known that anyone having a good crossbred, preferably of Percheron and Thoroughbred breeding, could almost always find a sale with the fire department. But, even so, the number of proper replacements was still a problem. There were just not enough horses of the exacting requirements now recognized by the buyers for the department.

At first horses were bought through the sealed bid method, but on one occasion all bids were found to be above that set by the supervisors. This resulted in the centering of the entire buying from one dependable market. Once the requirements of crossbreeding were permanently settled, the department decided to do something about it.

James B. Haggin and Lloyd Tevis were owners of considerable acreage near Bakersfield, where they specialized in breeding fine horses. Their Percherons were well known, as were their Thoroughbreds and Standardbreds. Here was the perfect place to set up a special crossbred program for the Fire Service. Haggin and Tevis already had several hundred horses—mostly purebred Percherons, Thoroughbred steeplechase stallions, and Standardbred American trotting stallions. To meet the unusual demands and standards now required for the department they began to breed the great Percheron mares to the racing stallions. The result was the perfect firehorse; exactly what the department had searched for so long and so far.

After establishment of a precise breeding program, the animals purchased from Haggin and Tevis were mostly unbroken four-year-old colts. Before purchase they were also run at set distances to test their wind. Some of these horses at the Bakersfield ranch were so

sensitive to the tests, that in the report of the famous veterinary surgeon, William F. Eagen, it was shown that some of them lost sixty pounds overnight after their rugged workout.

However, every animal raised for this special use did not get to the Fire Department. But once the cross-breeding was understood, the number of acceptable colts increased, because established breeding patterns were followed. Occasionally a filly of the intelligence and stamina required was used, but mainly the requirements were for geldings. They were full of spirit when they finally arrived at the Fire Department training stable, and there is a record of one kicking a telephone off the wall and doing several hundred dollars worth of damage before being subdued and harnessed. Later the colt became one of the best horses in the department. Apparently, after running his young days in pasture, the

An engine company of the San Francisco Fire Department, sixty years ago.

—Courtesy, San Francisco Fire Museum.

30

idea of confinement did not set well with this equine athlete.

Raising and breeding firehorses became a coveted business, but Haggin and Tevis had the corner on the biggest breeding program. A lot of the service stock came from the famous Haggin-Grant Ranch, where North Sacramento stands today. Another fine strain of Percheron stock came from the Obe Lowe's Ranch in Woodland, California. Haggin was constantly on the lookout for better stock and more than once he turned to Lowe to improve the crossbred strain. Sometimes the chief's horse was not as powerful as the service animals, but they all were required to have great speed, and here the Standardbred cross was introduced.

Assistant Chief Thomas Townsend drove a horse, named after him, to a four-wheeled, rubber-tired buggy. Townsend gave the chief a lot of grief because he fre-

Closeup of an early steam "pumper." Note the shining nickel and brass. The apparatus at the fire station were always immaculately maintained.

—Courtesy, San Francisco Fire Museum.

quently ran away, almost every second or third day. When he decided to run, there was no holding him. And he could trot faster than the average horse could run. However, there was no meanness about him, and he appeared to enjoy these dashes of speed. These attributes alone were enough to keep him in the service.

Firehorses were above the average in intelligence. They could sense a new man, and they weren't above taking advantage of him at every opportunity. One new man took a three-horse-hitch out for morning exercise. The cool, brisk air made the horses raring to go, and soon they were running away. The new driver, at their mercy, could only tug at the reins. An experienced fireman and driver, riding the rear platform, soon realized the predicament of the new man. He crawled up to the driver's seat, took the reins, and pulled the horses under control. That was the last time the new man ever drove a team.

There were men in the service who did nothing else but drive the horses. It was their responsibility to unhitch the horses at the scene of the fire and tie them safely out of the way until they were needed to remove the wagons again. There were times when the driver was as heroic as the fire fighters themselves. One day, going to a fire, a driver saw that, unless he did something drastic, there would be a collision with a street car, with resultant heavy loss of lives. Holding the reins firmly he drove the team through a plate glass window of a store on Market Street. The driver, getting the horses to their feet, discovered that one, named Sugar Dick, was the only one severely hurt. The animal was badly cut about his chest, and his jugular vein was severed. The driver, grasping the ends of the vein and holding them, shouted for a doctor. The policeman on the beat took out his gun to shoot Sugar Dick, but the doctor arrived, and told him to step aside. There was a short argument, but it stopped abruptly when the doctor insisted that this horse, a brave hero of the public, could be saved. Bystanders began to raise their voices in protest at the

32

policeman. He backed away to watch the doctor go to work.

Sugar Dick was sutured on the spot, sent to the lay-up stables, by horse ambulance, for a short period of convalescence, and then went back to work carrying some large scars to show for his experience. But for the driver, the animal might have bled to death on the spot.

These were the men the horses knew best. They understood the mischievousness of the animals, and enjoyed it most of the time. It broke the monotony of the daily routine of the service.

The firehorse was in essence an animal which worked where only the best could survive. His blood was important, and proved the need of breeding to a purpose. Mainly he needed to be strong of limb and wind, that he be obedient but fast. He was a warrior of fire, and for this hardy calling he did not shirk his duty. But as with every living thing he was not entirely infallible.

Abe Ruef was a chief's horse. He was dependable anywhere he was driven and under any conditions. He would stand for hours wherever the chief left him. But one day he fell from grace when a hay wagon stopped at the intersection where Abe was standing. As it paused at the corner he reached forward to take a few nibbles of hay. When the hay wagon started up again Abe was so engrossed in the tasty hay he forgot all about staying put, and followed it away.

The old style firehorse had an intelligence of his own. He had a trait of understanding that was remarkable, and his power to produce speed when it was needed saved many seconds that meant the difference between the life and death of a fire. His sense of responsibility was unlimited. He knew when to break his gaits. He sensed the danger of turning corners too sharp, and knew the hazards of a down-hill slope. To the well-trained firehorse a huge, ungainly truck, even over a bad route, was generally handled as easily as a light carriage.

However, there were instances where the right job had to be found for certain individual horses. The ani-

33

mals that did pass all the tests for department use were still individuals, and worked best where all conditions suited them. Gold Brick was one of these.

He was a beautiful chestnut, typically tight-skinned and rippling with smooth muscles. Because he was unusually fast, he was offered for a chief's buggy, but no one could hold him. He was then tried on a hose cart— on the nigh side. Here he was sluggish and slow. Puzzled, the trainers were about to return him to the main stables as unfit, when someone suggested moving him to the off side. He worked fine, and never again was there a complaint about his service. But he was a strange horse.

He never made friends with anyone, and disliked being petted. The men noticed that he was interested when they played cards. In this firehouse the lounge room was at the back of the firehouse and next to Gold

Horses coming out of stalls toward harness. A magnificent example of teamwork between men and animals. The horses many times were out and ready before the men could reach the bottom of the pole, or could get their own suspenders in place.

—Courtesy, San Francisco Fire Museum.

34

Brick's stall. He would stand looking out of his stall, his ears alert, as long as they played. He never went to sleep as long as they dealt the cards. He was always one of the first horses under harness. When rushing down the street he refused to step on manhole covers, jumping them, and doing the same for even the shadows of telephone poles. Dependable always, but he knew what he wanted to do.

During the whole life of duty, a firehorse served only at the wagon assigned him. Because, generally, the horse is a great creature of habit, and once learned never forgets, he was never moved except in cases of emergency. Each firehorse had his own specific place under the harness and to the one type of engine. Training and routine did the rest. Once trained he knew what was required of him and did it with the least effort and the greatest speed. He was always the picture of eagerness.

The "quick response." This view not only indicates the speed with which horses and men could ready themselves for a fire dash, but shows in detail the drop harness and split collars poised and ready for instantaneous coupling.

—Courtesy, San Francisco Fire Museum.

No. 15
QUICK RESPONSE

In short, he was a working racehorse rushing to save life and property.

Never again in the history of firefighting will there ever be such an animal, nor an era of such dash and excitement. The firehorse was loved by the neighborhood, a constant thrill to the children. He left many a spectator with a feeling of awe, and an emotion that brought a tear to the eyes of all those watching him gallop down the street, his ears back, his nostrils flared, and his eyes bright with the excitement of his work. The horse was a true crusader against the God of Fire.

THE GOULD ENGINE
A cross-section drawing.

36

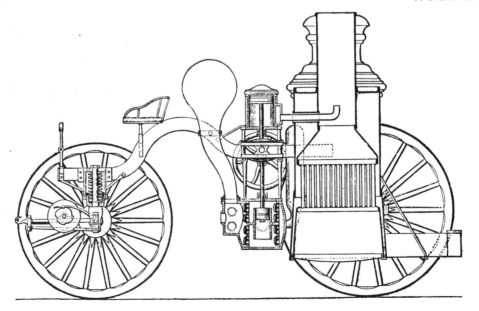

Training the Firehorse

BREAKING HORSES for fire service meant hours of hard work and patience, but once the animal had learned what was expected of him he never forgot. The trainers took great pride in their jobs because the end result helped make history for the service, a reputation of efficiency that made one firehouse or another outstanding. There was competition between the houses, which made the training itself precise and exacting. In fact the competition added greatly to the efficiency of the department.

After the young two-year-olds had been tested for stamina and soundness at the Haggin-Tevis Ranch, the future firehorses were sent to the San Francisco service's stables—directly to the superintendent, for observation. Here the horse remained for a brief session of training, which included the basics of harnessing, acquaintance with bells, and then the basic routine of the firehouse. He was then given a number, and entered into the books of the firehouse roster. When he reached this point he was fairly well on his way. Not until then was he assigned to a firehouse.

Notice was then chalked up on the alarm board of the prospective firehouses announcing that a new horse was arriving for training, to replace a retiring one. The next morning the department veterinary surgeon would drive up to the firehouse, the new horse with his bridle

strapped to the back of the buggy, trotting along behind.

Let us take one particular horse, and go through the training with him. Our horse is a fine looking bay named Cap, about sixteen hands in height, maybe two or three years old, bred of a Percheron mare and a Thoroughbred stallion.

"His name is Cap," the veterinarian said, undoing the straps and bringing him into the stable. "Plenty of spirit, and real bright too. We've got him accustomed to the sudden bells, lights, noises we use down at headquarters. He'll do all right here, I think. He'll not scare easily. Shouldn't be any trouble to break in."

Cap was taken in hand by the fireman who had been appointed by the chief, to the coveted job of training. Cap was to be his horse as long as he kept the animal properly groomed and cared for. And woe to any man who upset his daily routine, or made a play for the

A two-wheeled hose-cart. Note single horse, and rubber tires. One of the first horse drawn vehicles used in San Francisco.

—Courtesy, San Francisco Fire Museum.

38

horse's affections. A bitter fight was sure to result if a fireman discovered his horse being fed or petted by another member of his company.

The new horse was temporarily kept in the rear of the stable, in a stall normally used as a sick bay whenever one of the horses had a mild ailment. First, Cap was simply made comfortable in his new home, while his new master lavished kindness and attention on him. Cap also got acquainted with his co-workers, both men and horses, and began hearing, for the first time, the strange sounds that were to be so much a part of his life. First the small bells, then the loud ones, and the opening of doors, and the pounding of hoofs across the floor, the shouting of men, the rumble of heavy wheels, and then a silence in the whole house. And he would be left alone for a while. It all seemed strange and difficult to the new and naturally nervous animal.

Glistening engine, with its three-horse team. Because center of gravity was low, the engine could make the curves and turns with safety and speed.

—Courtesy, San Francisco Fire Museum.

On the third day the old horse was backed out of his stall by the fireman who had always taken care of him.

"You're going to be good about this now, aren't you?" The old horse was walked out of the stable into the yard. Neither of them would have been happy at the sight of a stranger in the old stall. It was as hard on a man as on the horse when a change was necessary. Now the young horse was led into the stall, and his bit was tied to the forward edge of the wall adjacent to the double doors that faced the apparatus room. Suddenly, with a startling zoom, the door sprung open. Standing out there, in front of Cap, was his friend. He stepped up to ease the animal's fright. He patted him gently, and gave him a carrot. The doors closed and, after a while, sprung open again. This exercise continued about a half hour in the morning, and was repeated in the afternoon.

Early on the morning of the fourth day Cap was again led into the old horse's stall, and the drilling began in earnest. The man at the desk simulated an alarm by tapping the bell several times with a screw driver. He then pulled the cord that struck the house gong, and the doors of the stall were sprung open. Cap's friend was standing there, as before, but this time the fireman stepped quickly forward and unclipped the strap that held the bit to the stall—and at that precise instant, another fireman, in the back of the stall, slapped the horse's rump with a shingle, and the startled animal bolted forward and was guided down the floor between the apparatus to the front of the steam engine. There he was halted beside the raised pole and swinging harness. After being held at that position for half a minute or so he was turned about and taken back through the passageway to the open stable in the rear, and led into the same stall again.

The exercise was repeated—until he came out of the stall with a leap. For the rest of the first week Cap was ·drilled in this manner, over and over again, until there was no necessity of leading him back and forth. Thus far he had learned to be alert at the sound of the small bell, and he stamped the floor in expectation when the loud bell struck. No longer did anyone have to wallop him with a shingle when the doors swung open. And his friend now waited for him across the room, at the front of the engine.

During the second week Cap got to know the two horses who would run at his sides. Every time his doors opened, their doors opened also, and all three trotted up to the front at the same time. For several days there was confusion and some fear in all of them; the young horse because he had yet to learn his job, and the other two because of the stranger in the middle. They resented his presence, and tried nipping him when he tried to get into position, until the fireman scolded them severely. But there were always three firemen standing up front to help the horses find their positions, and before long the operation was being done smoothly.

Learning to sidestep and back into place without disturbing the harness was the biggest trick of all. A clumsy push against the pole could upset the careful balance of the suspended harness and in an instant flip the taut straps overhead into a heap on the floor. It was particularly difficult for the horse in the middle, for he had to be exactly placed between the two poles, one of which was raised so he could step under it into position.

As the horses left their stalls, the outside right runner came trotting against Cap and then ran down close beside him, almost as though they were tied together. This meant they had to become accustomed to each other, and most compatible, because incompatible animals would have slowed the flight. It was very important to find animals who would give full tolerance to each other and become good running mates, as well as to find the best working position for each animal. They learned to run up to the front, slow down and stop, flank against flank, and then Cap would side-step under the raised pole with the help of some gentle nudging on the part of the outside horse until they were both in place. The

third horse would run down on the opposite side of the engine, and back into his outside left position. The old horse had taught the two outside runners a good deal about this maneuver, and now they, in turn, were helping to teach Cap.

Cap became one of the department's finest, and was one horse who thought for himself. However, he learned the hard way. One day, going to a fire, he came to a depression in the pavement. He jumped into it and went headlong to his knees. Five tons of equipment and the other horses pushed him for fifty feet along the pavement. He never trusted puddles again. He jumped every one he met, regardless of how small they might be. This was a feat in itself when one stops to realize he was between two giant horses with 10,000 speeding pounds behind him, and a pair of banging, battering poles that made a good aim impossible.

The company, with its two matched teams of grays.
—Courtesy, San Francisco Fire Museum.

42

Cap made two jumps that were well remembered. Usually, coming back from a fire, if the road was clear, the horses were let out a bit. This particular night the driver, after letting the horses out, noticed a barrel sitting over a manhole. It was too late to stop. He closed his eyes and waited as the horse rushed toward it. Cap jumped, and the fire engine completely demolished it.

Another night they were racing along the street car tracks. The driver did not see the two small red lights straight ahead, set out as danger signals marking a three feet drain ditch that had been dug across the street. Suddenly he felt the reins slack, and then the collars tighten, as all three horses jumped simultaneously. Sometimes there was no accounting for their ability to judge and make decisions.

The fire companies near Chinatown always knew when there was a fire in that location. Even before the

Crew pose with newer and later model steam pumper.

—Courtesy, San Francisco Fire Museum.

alarm was sent in. The Chinese all carried police whistles and when fire was discovered they would blow them for all they were worth. Immediately the firehorses nearby would begin to prance and snort, and by their actions demand that they be allowed out for harnessing. The men got so they recognized their alarm and they were ready to go before the tapper sounded the exact location of the fire.

Some horses were given vacations, but it was such a bore to them that many stole away and came back to stand in their regular places. Yet another horse, when his guard rope was down, quietly stole away from his engine house and made his way to the department's stables. He found an empty stall, and lay down for the rest he must have felt he needed.

Excitement hit the horses just as it did the men. At night, when the bell struck, and the horses were lying in their stalls, they would be on their feet at the first tap, and out of their stalls and under the harness by the time the men were ready to make the hitch. They would stand, restless, anxious, and waiting to go.

The firehorse had a hard life. But, like with Cap, it was a life he was used to, and he did not want to change it. Even though Cap spent half his existence in a stall, waiting, as did the men, for the bell to hit, it was evident and true that the fire service got into the blood of both horses and men. And, indeed, once a firehorse—he remained so until he died. Cap was no exception.

The Care of the Horses

The routine of caring for horses in the old days was strict and careful, and under the constant supervision of superior officers. Each day the regular allowance of cooked grain for the horses was set aside by the driver. At one o'clock in the morning, the assistant house watchman was required to pour boiling water over the grain in a bucket, and then fix the cover on tightly so as to prevent the escape of the steam. On feeding the first batch to the horses about 5:30 A.M. another batch was immediately prepared. A handful of salt had to be thrown into the oats while they were steaming. Should this be forgotten, the fireman soon knew it, for the horses would refuse to eat. A full bucket of water had been given at 5 A.M., and it was repeated again at 6 P.M., after another bucket of water.

However, the foremost thing in every horse's life was not food. Billy the Goat loved one particular fireman. He was a fine, rangy roan. He knew his driver's voice, and just the sound of it was enough to make him excited. He refused to respond to anyone else, and became quite unruly if anyone else tried to handle him. Once he bolted away from another driver, and ran back to the old engine to stand trembling beside his former master. This proved that it was difficult to be even a relief horse.

Billy was one of the service's finest, so there was no question of what to do. He was restored to his former

driver in the old routine, and served many years more without further trouble.

But, Billy was an exception, because food holds an important place in any animal's life. The firehorses were always bedded down in clean straw, with an allowance of hay and usually a few carrots.

The reason for this far spaced feeding was the condition of the animal. At no time was he stuffed with food. By spacing his feedings, no man had "it all" to do, nor was any horse loggy. But there was another purpose for the well-being this feeding schedule brought the horses. The horses rarely got a good night's sleep, because each time an alarm was sent in, no matter from where, all horses were released from their stalls and stood under the harness until either hooked up for the run, or released because the call was not from their district. Later

The pride of the service— glittering engine — glistening horses — and firemen dressed for parade.

46

the alarm system was improved, so that only the departments needed were aroused.

Sometimes when returning to the stable after a fire, a horse would deliberately make his way to the stall of another animal. The rightful occupant of the stall would attempt to drive off the intruder and a real fight of biting, pawing and squealing would result—much like mischievous children who haven't had their energy expended. But at the roar of the driver, "Get out of there!" the invading horse would scamper to where he belonged. It was never necessary to lay a hand on him.

All horses were exercised for an hour a day, unless a run had been made after 1 A.M. In good weather the horses were permitted to stand outside their engine houses, hooked up to the apparatus, from 9:45 to 11 A.M. Sometimes they were allowed to be tied in back of the firehouse, but only two or three horses at a time to avoid

Engine, with team of bays. Note the draft and weather shield around the fire box.

—Courtesy, San Francisco Fire Museum.

confusion if a bell sounded. It was necessary to be aware of emergencies at all times.

One day a horse was allowed out of his stall to sun himself in front of the engine house. The chief arrived to inspect the horses, and wanted to know why the animal was allowed out when the gong might ring at any moment. He was assured that the horse knew what he was doing. There was an argument—the driver insisting that the animal was dependable, and the chief just as certain that no horse was entirely trained to think. He kept shaking his head with disapproval. Finally, to prove his point, a fireman rang the gong. The horse hurried into place, and the chief came away with a few bruises because he didn't get out of the way of one firehorse who knew his job and did it well.

However, all was not pleasant for the firehorse. There were many stable fires, and these upset the firehorses when they arrived on the scene to hear their brothers screaming in fear and pain. At these times they were hard to manage. Even the men were terribly upset, and it was not unusual to see a fireman with tears in his eyes.

While most of the horses were loved, and given the best of care there were a few isolated cases of mistreatment. Teasing or annoying a horse, teaching it tricks, was strictly condemned. However, despite the intelligence of the horses some became outlaws because of the abuse and teasing. It takes much time and patience to train a horse well, but it can be quickly undone with mistreatment. Such horses were dangerous and hard to control. Thirteen hundred pounds is a lot of muscle and strength.

It took a good driver to handle these big horses at a full gallop. Drivers of any horse drawn apparatus were always strapped in before leaving the firehouse. These were strict orders from the chief engineer of the department. There were no exceptions. Even the gentlest horses became difficult when the bell rang.

Character traits were common discussion when the subject was about the firehorses. Pay Day was a problem, although a powerful horse. At the sound of the gong, when he was released from his stall, he would back his hind quarters close to the brass sliding pole and kick at the men as they slid down. Shoeing him was a violent affair. He had to be trussed and swung up in a sling. No matter what was wanted of him he did the opposite. If his drinking water wasn't the right temperature he kicked the bucket over.

Taken ill, one day, Pay Day was tied out in the stable yard to a snubbing post. Later in the day he was found dead, lying in a tangled mass of ropes, with one tightly wound around his neck. He had battered his head against the iron snubbing post and hung himself. But even if a horse did have some unpleasant traits, his worth to the department, many times, kept him in service. His care still was the best.

No gas or electric lights were allowed to be placed or kept lighted in front of a horse's eyes at night. Muzzles were forbidden, between the hours of six at night and six in the morning, except when standing on the street at a fire. Horses were never fed when they were warm. After a run, their mouths and nostrils were always sponged with cold water, and they were never given more than two or three swallows of water at such a time.

Upon returning from an alarm, the rules called for the washing and examination of the horse's feet for loose shoes or nails. Then they were rubbed down and blanketed. Because speed was the essence, bits were always kept in the horse's mouth, with the exception of feeding time. A team could be ready to go in 7½ seconds. Even though the horses were given a number when first purchased, they were more than numbers to the men. In the record book was also recorded a brief history of each animal. Sometimes, this was a help in choosing a name. And, indeed, almost every horse was given a name by the men in the firehouse to which he was assigned.

Horse No. 742 on the books was a beautiful, satin-coated brown animal called Jimmie. He was a trotter

with a great reputation, and was used on the Chief's buggy. Soon after his purchase he fell, and dislocated a hip. For three months he was kept off his feet by means of a sling. Six months after the first accident Jimmie fell again, breaking his other hip, and again he went in for treatment. Contrary to belief, every horse who breaks a leg is not shot. Much depends on where the break is, and how much damage is done to the bone ends. No animal was destroyed if he could be saved. However, with Jimmie's second accident the chief despaired of ever driving him again.

Yet, strange as it may seem when you consider the general theory that horses are never truly useful after broken bones, Jimmie came back, and was in service for years after that. It was the quick action of the firemen in getting Jimmie into a sling, before he threshed around

Water Tower No. 1, San Francisco Fire Department. Firehouses needed depth to house this new and sophisticated equipment.

—Courtesy, San Francisco Fire Museum.

50

and caused the broken bone to be so damaged to a point beyond knitting, that probably saved his life.

The men worried about their horses, and sometimes it was questioned as to who got the best care, the men *or* the horses. In cold weather the chill had to be taken off their drinking water. On cold or stormy nights, when it was necessary that a team remain at a fire, the driver was required to blanket and exercise them every half hour for ten minutes, by leading them up and down the street.

With three horses under his care the driver was always kept busy for the duration of the fire with the welfare of the animals. While at the fire, the horses were unhitched and taken a safe distance away from the burning buildings. At the firehouse, their care was never neglected at any time. They were catered to like prima donnas.

Horse drawn Fire Truck No. 3, Pacific Avenue. Photo taken September 17, 1912.

—Courtesy, San Francisco
Fire Museum.

The rear door of the house had to be kept closed, so no drafts could sweep through. The front door, was left unlocked, and a fireman sat in a strategic spot in the firehouse where he could observe most of what went on. These watches were lonely, and sometimes the fireman would doze at his post. Even this did not escape the wise firehorse.

Mush was a dappled gray who teamed with two other handsome grays, Pup and Bob. They pulled the engine on Bush Street. Mush was known as a character. He was playful, affectionate and mischievous. He refused to stay in his stall, and knew how to open the chain. These three were the pick of the department, with their massive muscles bulging under their heavy, velvety skins. But Mush was the clown.

He could move his heavy body in a soundless way, and many nights no one knew of his prowling until the crash of a bucket gave him away. He loved to steal up to a snoozing fireman, and nuzzle him vigorously before the man could ward him away. He was game to the core, yet gameness caused his disgrace, and everyone believed him to be a quitter until the day came when it was all explained.

It was a third alarm fire. Mush and his team-mates were off, straining at their collars. Across the steep hills, the bumpy car tracks and around sharp corners the heavy engine, behind them, bounding along under their massive power. Down a steep grade they went. A narrow corner came up in front of them, and they made a sharp swerve to one side of the slippery street. Mush went down. He stumbled to his feet and they went on as if nothing had happened. But on the return to the firehouse the driver noticed that Mush's head was drooping, and he walked with lagging steps, as if his feet were made of lead.

From then on he was a changed horse. He lost his desire for action. All he seemed to want was to return from a fire, not to go to one. For a while everyone thought he had lost interest, and some called him a quit-

52

ter, but his driver knew this was not the cause. Mush's animation was gone, and he was no longer mischievous. This was not the old Mush. The driver insisted the department's veterinarian examine him. The department felt badly when the veterinarian discovered a badly damaged heart caused by undue strain.

A few days later Mush dropped dead in the stables. The word among the firemen was that Mush had given his heart to the department, and for many years his silvery tail hung in a glass case on the wall of the old firehouse on Bush Street. But Mush's experience was unusual. The horses were checked as often as a baby.

At unannounced times, the assistant chief made rounds of the house to look over the horses. He would pull a white silk handkerchief from his pocket, and rub it over the back, neck and sides of the horses. Any slight soil on the silk was serious; a real offense. A complaint about the care of the horses meant a fine of at least ten days' pay. Cleanliness was important, but much attention was also paid to the feet of the animals. Without good, healthy feet a horse was useless. Shoes were changed approximately every four weeks.

Perhaps the kind of treatment given the animals by the superintendent of the stables was well demonstrated by a big, blazed-faced horse belonging to Engine No. 6. On two occasions, when he had been sent to the lay-up stables for a rest, he left, made his way back to his own firehouse at midnight. The front door of the firehouse had been left open as usual, and he had no trouble making his escape. The men at the firehouse heard him outside, and waited to see what he would do. He went straight to his old stall and settled down comfortably.

When an animal worked his best under harness the men took every precaution to keep him comfortable and safe. They spent many hours figuring the solution to whatever problem was at hand.

Fanny was a large mare standing fifteen hands high. She was a showy animal, with a stripe down her nose and four white stockings. She knew the rules of the de-

partment as well as the men. She was ten years old, and
had been with the service for a long time. But every
night about midnight she would begin to snort and paw
as if she were running. She would breathe fast and
hard, her eyes would be wide open but, actually, she
was fast asleep. The men were afraid to awaken her for
fear she would injure herself. They widened her stall
for safety. Early one morning, while having one of her
dreams, she jumped to her feet and ran to her place be-
neath the harness. Then she awakened, and she sensed
she had put herself in a ridiculous situation, her head
drooped, her ears fell forward, and she ran back to
her stall.

Each horse had his own large and airy stall. The animal's comfort was all important. One of the horses never
laid down to sleep and was constantly falling to his
knees. It frightened him and made him nervous. The

*Engine No. 11, San Fran-
cisco Fire Department. A
call out at night, April 1914.*

54

men devised a canvas sling, and the horse found he could back up and rest his haunches on the reinforced canvas. Many people came to see the horse who slept sitting down. Not even ropes or halters encumbered the fire-horse. When the bell rang, the horses could be out of their stalls and under harness at the first tap. Even though they were restless and eager to go, they always waited for the commands. Their obedience was a splendid thing to see.

The men discovered the horses couldn't be fooled. These big animals could tell the difference between an alarm coming in or when the bell hit for the time signal. If the bell hit for an alarm test they would come leisurely out of their stalls, but if it was the fire alarm they came quickly to their feet at the sound of the telephone. Strange to say, better time was made at night than in the daytime, and it could never be explained.

Ladder company, complete with ready men and tin hats, pose in front of fire station. The "pep boy," in straw hat and glasses, not identified.

In one firehouse the men swore they had the noisiest horses in the department. Brownie pawed, Mike whinnied constantly, and Trix chewed on the wood of her stall. This particular night the horses were noisier than usual. Brownie pawed so violently that one of the men went over to his stall to scold him, and then noticed that the animal kept looking across the street. When the fireman went to investigate he discovered the newspaper presses were on fire. Looking through the windows they discovered the building full of smoke. There was the beginning of flames. The fire was out almost before the alarm was turned in. Once back at quarters Brownie had his morning oats, Mike whinnied, and Trix chewed on her stall, and all was normal again.

But, nevertheless, the firehorse led a hard life. Half his life was spent standing in a stall, waiting, as did the men, for the bell. Indeed, the fire service is akin to gold fever. For the men, they seemed never to want to be free of it. Training, routine and habit completely influenced the horses. Habit was so strong that they would run back into their own burning stables, because its familiar surroundings had always promised sanctuary. The animal's one track mind told him he would be safe. But besides this homing instinct, these horses were bred for endurance.

Rosie proved this point. She lived the hard life of the firehorse, but she proved that stamina was bred into the animal. When she was ordered to retire at the age of twenty-four she emphasized this trait by living another ten years.

The horses were always alert, and knew what was going on. They were really never off duty. Many times they would awaken the watchman when he went to sleep if a stranger walked in. They made a warning racket with their pawing and neighing. They were true servants of the service, and precaution was never denied for an instant. Twice a day saw practice in every firehouse, and if a horse could not have gotten away to a fire within the limits of these tests, he might well have torn up his stall and everything in sight.

It was a matter of training and constant routine. Although the horse knew the difference between morning and afternoon tests, in comparison to the real thing, he was so eager to perform that no trouble was ever experienced. Their training would have and did carry them right into the jaws of death if called upon to do so.

THE BUTTON FIRE ENGINE
Weight up to three tons.
Could throw a stream 200 feet.

The Care of the Horses

IT TOOK A CERTAIN kind of man to be a fireman. So, what of the men who became firemen and worked with the horses? All the men who went into the service were not horsemen. Some were drivers, but there were those known as "herders" who knew little about horses, and through ignorance did not consider the horses an important part of the service. Men, who were careless about driving the horses were usually brutal, not because they disliked the animals, but because they did not understand that handling horses took a special talent.

Horses had likes and dislikes, and could be temperamental. To an experienced horseman, this was not a sign of meanness. However, most drivers cared well for their horses because they were an important part of their lives. They were deserving of the best. Because the horses were naturally highstrung due to the life they led, they especially resented brutal treatment.

Good drivers made certain their horses were fed, watered and groomed often. Meticulously, after a fire, they were carefully sponged about the mouth and nostrils to remove the smoke dust. To the animals this was as refreshing as a bath. It was important to be clean, not only for the health of the animal, but because comfort promised placidness.

Volunteer Fire Helmet of Lafayette Hook and Ladder Company No. 2, organized in San Francisco in 1853.

—Courtesy, History Room,
Wells Fargo Bank.

During the summer months a driver would wash his horse's stalls down daily. He would constantly inspect their feet. Many times a driver was so particular that he would pack their feet with Denver mud not less than twice a month. They well knew that a moist hoof did not crack, and the Denver mud kept the hoofs from becoming dry and brittle. It was important to keep the hoofs from breaking off because they held the nails better. Also, this kept the shoes from becoming loose and possibly lost, and eliminated many shoeing problems.

Each fireman was responsible for the shoeing of the animals in his care. He watched how the shoes wore, and usually asked the farrier (horseshoer) to shoe the horses in his care every four weeks on the average. Besides taking pride in the care of his animals, a lost or loose shoe meant direct return to the firehouse, and a piece of equipment out of service. There was a never ending effort to improve the service; to make it faster and more efficient.

A weekly inspection was held, in the old horse-drawn apparatus days, to determine how quickly horses could be harnessed to the engines. The battalion chief of the district stood with a stop watch in his hand and checked the time. A firehouse's reputation was only as good as its horses and its men.

If it took more than twelve seconds for the men to harness up and be at the curb line of the street, it was considered poor time. One might say here that they rolled out of quarters quicker with the horses than they do with the motor apparatus today. But today, of course, the time is made up on the road.

It was possible to hitch up three horses and be outside the quarters in *less* than twelve seconds. First of all there were about ten or twelve men on duty in each company. The driver, on the sound of the alarm, would dash to his seat and strap himself in. The bits were always in the horse's mouths, except at feeding time, so many seconds were saved in not having to bit the horses. The bridle snaps at the end of the reins were carefully hung on the open collars, accessible in a second, for snapping on to the bit rings. Each man had a horse to hook up.

In the case of a three-horse hitch, three men were at their posts immediately at the first tap of the bell. Each snapped a collar over the neck of one of the animals as it was led or moved into place. Many of the horses ran by themselves into position when released from their stalls, and there were not a few who could release their own stall chains.

As the collar was snapped, each man, grabbing the two hanging reins, snaps in each hand, hooked them into the large rings of the bit. Then drivers and horses and men were on their way. The reputation of every driver was inseparably with that of his team. He shared with the glory of the great run or the humiliation of a poor showing.

A competitive, or speed test was held April 22, 1893 to ascertain the exact time in which one man could dress, harness the horses and have the engine in the street after the gong sounded. At this test, Lemuel Rudolph of No. 7 Engine, carried off the prize, which was a twelve pound molded silver eagle. He won it by making a hitch in $25\frac{1}{2}$ seconds. There was some discussion that John Brophy, who got second prize, should have won first. At the house of Engine No. 14, he was dressed, had three horses hitched and was in the driver's seat and had driven thirty-odd feet into the street. His time was 26 seconds. But Brophy's quarters had no sliding pole and he had to run down a flight of twenty-seven steps. This, the judges finally decided, was what made the difference in timing, and Rudolph kept the trophy.

When the horse was introduced into the fire service and became an important part of it there also began one of the most romantic eras for this animal. Every department was sure they had the finest and the best of stock. Perhaps in the history of the firehorse, the two greatest animals ever known to the service were Dan and Joe. The year was 1885. This pair of horses had everything—intelligence, endurance and speed. They brought back

61

many trophies from London, England and Paris, France, where they gave exhibitions of their speed and efficiency. Dan was killed in a collision with a street car while dashing to a fire. Joe lived on, to be turned out to pasture.

As the result of an argument as to Joe's ability to remember the old days, he was brought into the station by the chief. He had been away from the service for five years. He was placed in a stall, the gong was hit, and out Joe came to take his place under the harness as if he'd never been away. He proved the point of argument, and was returned to his comfortable pasture, where he died a year later. Joe also proved that once a horse learns something well, he never forgets. He was mounted by a taxidermist, and placed in the city museum, where he was on view for many years.

In 1904 a battalion chief timed a crew hitching a team and getting out of the firehouse. His report showed the time required, on apparatus floor, to hitch up three horses, as 7½ seconds. Three horses, standing at the poles, were hitched in four seconds. There were all kinds of tests, and all kinds of records. Indeed, besides the constant attempt to improve the efficiency of the department there were many things done to break the monotony and tediousness of constant surveillance for the firefighters.

The driver had the hardest job in the service. He was the first man up in the morning, and the last one to bed at night. Three times a week the horses were taken out at 5 A.M. for exercise, unless they had run the night before. This meant the driver got up at 4 A.M. There were stalls to clean and horses to groom and harness to polish. This all had to be finished by 10 A.M. Otherwise 6 A.M. was the usual rising hour for all firemen. Upon rising, the driver curried and brushed his horses, while another scrubbed down the stalls with boiling water, and a third man took care of the harness. Still others took care of the specific feeding routine.

Each fireman who had the care of a horse went back to do his final chore for the day before retiring. He cleaned the stall floor, and bedded it with straw or peat moss. He filled the wire basket with hay, and put water in the basin on the left wall. Also, at 10 A.M. every morning there was uniform inspection, and examination of quarters, horses and apparatus. During these inspections the men stood at attention, while the captain walked about. If all was satisfactory, the men were saluted and were released to go at will to quarters.

They looked forward to the leisure time after inspection. Unless they were called, their time was their own, to do as they wished. Some slept, others read, and almost always was there some kind of a card game in progress.

They worked twenty-four hours a day under the old system, with only one day off each month. The hours were long and tedious. The driver had the day watch from 6 A.M. to 6 P.M., the lieutenant from 6 P.M. to 10

P.M. Then the night watch was given over to the regular firemen on four-hour shifts. Occasionally a watchman fell asleep in his chair. This was strictly against the rules. Each fireman knew he owed much of his reputation to the horses. More than once they created such a disturbance that the fireman woke up at once. After 5 A.M. no watchman ever fell asleep, for the horses knew the time, and they pawed in their stalls for breakfast.

McKinlay was an attentive animal, whose stall was near the grain chute. He watched the man on duty measure the grain every day. One day he manipulated the chain across his stall and, stepping lightly, went over toward the chute. Having managed this chute door previously, a fireman, duly warned, decided to tip a chair against the wall and sleep there to catch the culprit red-handed. McKinlay eased over to the chute soundlessly and wiggled the trap door with his muzzle. The chute led from the floor above, where the grain was stored loose instead of in sacks. Finally, McKinlay released the catch, and the grain poured down until the fireman was almost smothered. McKinlay hurried back to his stall, and the men spent the rest of the night bucketing the grain back up the stairs. Even though it was an annoyance, the whole thing was treated as a joke, and the chair-tipping fireman took much ribbing from his fellow workers about the soundless horse. This was typical of the attitude of the men in regard to the horses.

Teddy was another firehorse who was well acquainted with the grain chute. The men began to notice that he was gaining weight. There had to be a reason. At first the men thought he was stealing into another stall and pushing the occupant away from his ration of grain. They set about to watch him, and discovered he was slipping out of his stall to get an extra helping of grain from the chute. Unlike McKinlay, he was able to manipulate the chute door open just enough to get the extra grain and yet not so far as to allow the door to get out of control. Apparently after he was satisfied with the extra portion, he slipped back again. Besides the big interest in food, there were many things to upset the daily routine. In fact it kept the men busy trying to eliminate the disturbances caused by the horses.

There were horses who would stomp on the floor or pound their stall doors all night long. These horses were called "boilermakers," and they constantly disturbed the men's sleep. Many of the drivers would spend hours lying in wait trying to catch these culprits, but the horses were smart. They always seemed to sense the driver's presence. One driver rigged up a gallon can filled with bits of iron, attached to a cable. The cable was passed through two pulleys that were fastened to the ceiling, one end through a hole bored in the dormitory floor, right by the driver's bed. The ring on the end of the cable was placed over a hook. Every time one of the boilermakers started pounding his stall the driver would lift the ring from the hook and let the can strike the horse in the middle of the back, giving him a scare. Many times this acted as a cure, because the horse could not figure where the can came from and yet, every time he stomped, it hit him.

When the men succeeded in breaking an animal of a bad habit, they passed the disciplinary treatment on to the chief, who saw to it that the information was made general knowledge to all districts. Frequently the chief checked these methods before accepting them.

The chief was usually a man in his sixties, well-built and wearing, at least, a full mustache. Some had sideburns, and a few sported beards. The chief came up through the ranks. He would never send a man where he wouldn't go himself. And he was faithful to the horses of the fire service. Each chief had his own special buggy horse. Charlie was one of these.

He was pensioned after a long service and had been away for eleven years, but before his retirement he was known as the fastest horse to get under harness. Charlie was brought back to celebrate his chief's retirement, and, for a test. When they brought Charlie to the firehouse his mane was unkempt, his tail was tangled, and

his fetlocks were long and shaggy. The men cleaned and groomed him until he began to take on the old appearance, and they kept him hid until the chief arrived to say goodbye to the men and horses whom he had worked with through the years.

The men asked the chief to stand at one side for a surprise ceremony. They brought out the chief's buggy, shafts and harness lifted in the air and hanging in place. They left Charlie, standing loose, some fifty feet away. Someone sounded the gong. Quick as a flash the old horse leaped for the shafts, and the firemen snapped the harness into place. After eleven years the old horse hadn't forgotten. Standing there watching Charlie leap into the shafts, as in his active days, brought tears to the chief's eyes. The men had intended for the chief to jump into the buggy and drive off. Instead he stumbled forward and threw his arms around the old horse's neck

First three-horse hitch used in the San Francisco Fire Department.

—Courtesy, San Francisco Fire Museum.

66

and stood clinging to him with tears streaming down his face. Old Charlie had not been too old to respond to the service he knew so well. It was hard to retire the men, but worse for the horses, who never seemed to understand why they were sent away.

Firefighters know if they can get to work within five to six minutes of an outbreak of fire there is a ninety per cent chance it can be stopped. Ten minutes of unmolested fire in a basement may make it too late to save the rest of the building. Gusts of hot air rising through the building can, in a short time, generate other fires in the top floor of a building. It is then that a fire can become stubborn.

After some experience in battling flames the men would begin to know a few of the habits of a blaze. They would see in the color of the flames or the behavior of the smoke an underlying fierceness or mildness, that is

67

The *Eureka Engine Company. Photo taken in 1871.*

—Courtesy, History Room, Wells Fargo Bank.

not apparent to the general public. The smoke, at times, would be forced by the terrific heat below, and shoot straight up for some distance before it would be taken by the wind. Sparks, flaming shingles and pieces of clapboarding would explode upward through the smoke. The men would hold the hose and huddle up as close to the fire front as they could. Frequently there was a serious loss of hose, some had to be left behind, and some would burn while others would burst.

Sometimes the fierce heat would make the brass on the steamer too hot to touch. The firemen would be soaked to the skin by wind-blown hose streams, their eyes would be red and smarting while the sparks and embers showered like hail. But they would stay with it until the fire was in its final gasps. It was a fascinating life. And while most firemen went into the service because it was a job, it grew on them, became an important part of their lives. Yet, there were certain influences that brought other men to serve.

One fireman joined the service through an early experience. When a child, his mother put him in a buggy to sun on the porch. A woman escapee from the Contagion building across the street from the firehouse snatched the infant from the buggy and started running down the street. In those days the Contagion building was commonly called the Pest House, and although its original intent was for the housing of patients with communicable disease, it frequently housed mentally ill persons. The baby's mother screamed and started in pursuit, but the woman had too much of a start. The mother turned and ran to the firehouse next door, where her brother was a driver on Engine No. 25, and told him of the kidnapping. He hurriedly hitched up the fire engine, and, at top speed, went after the woman.

The woman was no match for the fast firehorses. After a three-block chase the fireman caught up with her, stopped the horses at the curb, and retrieved his nephew. A short time later he came trotting back to the firehouse with the baby propped up on the driver's seat, none the worse for wear. Hearing this story told and retold made up the mind of this one firefighter.

Many people loved the fire service, and frequently children were given the honor of being mascots of the firehouses in their neighborhoods. But it was not always the children who had this honor.

One famous mascot was Lillie Hitchcock Coit, who was chosen by the Knickerbocker Engine Company No. 5. She was a little older than most of the mascots, but she had such a passion for fires that it made an impression at the firehouse. She learned the routine so well that she went to as many of them as was possible. She made herself useful by manning the hose wagon.

Lillie was fifteen years old when she began her famous career with the Fire Department. One afternoon, during a fire on Telegraph Hill, the company was short-handed. The result of this shortage of manpower caused the company to fall behind on the way to the scene of the fire. Lillie was on her way home from school when she noted the plight of the Knickerbocker Company No. 5. Throwing her books to the ground she ran to a vacant place on the rope, pulling like a Trojan, with face flushed, and the determination of a Joan of Arc. She called to the bystanders for assistance with the words, "we'll beat them!" Many men came to the rescue at her calls, and like a red streak Knickerbocker No. 5 went up the slope to get first water. This was a great day for Lillie. From that day on she won the hearts of the volunteer firemen, and was a familiar part of Knickerbocker Company.

Her father had great difficulty in keeping her from running to fires. She was so fascinated by the red shirts the firemen wore that the company presented her with a red shirt, a helmet, and a number to wear. After she was made an honorary member of Engine No. 5 she wore the numeral as an ornament with her colorful costumes. There never was a parade in the city that Lillie Hitchcock Coit was not seen atop Knickerbocker Engine No. 5. Many gold badges were presented to her, and

she wore them all at one time or another. On her death she left one-third of her fortune to the city of San Francisco for use in the department. Several years after her death a memorial tower was erected in her honor, and as a tribute to the firemen of San Francisco. This tower would be a constant reminder of the girl who fought the fires.

Truck No. 5, Post and Fillmore Streets, in San Francisco, 1906.
—Courtesy, History Room, Wells Fargo Bank.

Tack and Shoeing

IN THE EARLY days the general stables were on what is known as Alamo Square, bounded by Steiner, Scott, Fulton and Hayes Streets. It was also the general repair shop. Later the stables were at Sixteenth and Valencia, adjacent to the old car barns, then at Jack Dalton's stables on Waller near Fillmore, and finally at Division between Tenth and Eleventh Streets. In this period there was not too much equipment to work with.

The fire engine, in the beginning, was drawn by a team, that is, after the rope-drawn, man-powered type. The hose wagon—usually a two-wheeled cart, bearing a large winding reel for the hose—could be drawn by a single horse at high speed. Many of the larger companies had more than one of these single horse affairs.

At this time all the apparatus came around the Horn to San Francisco. It took time to establish builders who could manufacture to order the wagons. These had to be able to stand up under extremely hard use. They needed to be substantial for the high speed that was the main part of every run. Indeed, speed was the essence, and every house appeared to have pride in maintaining that one attribute.

Many firefighters will tell you that the horses had a spirit of competition. They did not like their stablemates passing them. Because of this the drivers had to keep their equipment several feet apart. The net result of some of this unplanned competition was broken harness when the horses took it upon themselves to take first place. The harness, however, was simply made, so it was not difficult to replace.

The most important part of the harness arrangement was the collar. This was hinged on top and open at the bottom, just the reverse of the ordinary ones used on farm animals. An automatic device locked itself when the collar was snapped closed. When the horses left their stalls they were trained to place their necks close to the collars, and their haunches close to the breech straps. No belly straps were used on firehorses.

In the beginning the harness was kept on the horses constantly. They were untied by hand when the alarm sounded, and led to the apparatus. This was a slow process, so finally the harness was suspended on straps above so that when each horse was underneath the harness could be dropped into place.

In 1875 Edward O'Sullivan, a San Francisco fireman, patented and demonstrated his swinging harness, which consisted of four straps suspended from the four corners of the ceiling of the engine house. These straps supported the harness and had weights to regulate the various heights the equipment was to be held over the horses.

This invention was not only used here, but later in New York, Brooklyn and many other cities. In fact, it was the general type finally used throughout the world until the day when all departments became motorized. This harness swing was checked frequently.

The harness itself was as carefully tended as the horses. Harness makers were an important part of the department. The harness maker made regular visits to each firehouse, and tested straps and repaired those parts that had been patched by the men during an emergency, usually at the scene of a fire. Every firehouse had replacements of the various parts of the harness, constantly kept ready to use in case of such emergencies. Many times rivets were used by the men for a quick repair. The harness maker usually stitched all parts of the harness together with heavy linen thread. Simple, though it was, any worn part was immediately replaced on return to the firehouse. In case of too much wear, a whole new set was made. Extra heavy harness was used in the breaking and training, and when one thinks of 1300 pounds of muscle, coupled with a young spirited colt, it was no wonder that this was in constant need of repair.

The harness was daily cleansed with pure castile soap and water. At regular intervals all of it was treated with a special oil. The sweat and lather, that so badly dried and deteriorated the leather, was never allowed to dry after a run. Because of this special care, the leather always remained pliable, and the service got the ultimate use out of its harness. One of the familiar, pleasant smells of any firehouse, was the pungent odor of well-cared-for leather.

During the 1906 earthquake, amidst the excitement and confusion, Brownie, a chief's horse, broke his harness and disappeared. Two months later he was found pulling a vegetable wagon. He appeared docile, and didn't appear to mind his new job. The driver said he had found him wandering in the San Mateo hills. Because so much had been destroyed by the fire, the man didn't try to locate an owner. He was returned to the firehouse. He walked along quietly until he came in sight of his familiar home, then, he began to snort and prance. He was fitted with a new set of harness, and returned to his old stall.

Every bit as important as the harness was the type of shoe demanded by the San Francisco Fire Service. Cobblestones and slippery streets were as smooth as glass, and dangerous in times of speed. The shoes were most unusual. The heel part of the shoe was of corrugated rubber, attached to a piece of leather. The rubber pad formed a suction cup and a tread piece, assuring the animal of a firm footing on any kind of street. The steel part of the shoe was half sized, or in some cases a regular

iron shoe was nailed in place. It was nailed over the leather pad to the hoof. The shoes had no calks but did have a toe clip. The shoes were frequently examined for wear. Some animals wore the toes down, while others wore the shoes down at the sides. To prevent undue strain on the tendons and muscles of the legs meant that the shoes must be changed whenever they showed any signs of wear. Ordinarily, the shoes were changed every four weeks.

Sometimes the spirited animals didn't take to shoeing or clipping. A special harness was finally devised to lift the animal a few inches off the ground during the operation, which made them quite helpless. The old stables for the fire department were then provided with this special equipment for the clipping and shoeing of their horses.

Many methods were devised because each animal, being an individual, presented a different problem. Those

With clang, clatter and roar, the engine, with its magnificent three-horse team, departs a San Francisco firehouse to battle a blaze. Photograph, 1897.

—Courtesy, History Room,
Wells Fargo Bank.

74

who threshed around in the air were handled with a squeeze chute. There were many different methods of disabling by tying, and they were used until the animal accepted the farrier. However, these isolated cases were few. Most of the horses, when they discovered they would not hurt, handled very easily. There were a few scattered cases of plain meanness. The small number who were difficult to handle were usually those who were afraid.

On the whole the horses were given the best of care— equal to that of the finest, expensive, racing animal. Their welfare was the running gear of the service, and it was important to make their specialized care as easy on them as possible. The farriers, the harnessmakers and the trainers, the wagon builders and the veterinarians were looked upon with great respect. It was a privilege to be a part of a fire service such as San Francisco's well equipped department. And it took everyone working together to build such a service.

Knickerbocker No. 5. This manpower pump was one of the largest old side stroke fire engines ever made.

—Courtesy, History Room, Wells Fargo Bank.

To keep them in practice, the horses were hooked up three times a day—8 a.m., 12 m., 5 p.m.—at the stroke of the bell.

—Courtesy, History Room, Wells Fargo Bank.

Firehouses and Equipment

FIREHOUSES OF ANY size usually maintained from three to four different pieces of fighting equipment. The one most every person remembers, of that era, was the steam engine, which was used to pump water into the hoses. Here, the horses were used as a team, although many were harnessed three abreast. There was something of the spirit of the old Romans and their chariot races to see three horses dashing at breakneck speed, perfectly in step with each other, pulling the huge boiler, belching smoke and sparks as it rolled down the street.

The boiler always gleamed like silver. It looked like a smoke-stack sitting on a wagon base, but it was one piece of equipment that thrilled every child. Firehouses were known by the engine it housed, and the three horses who pulled it. This was one piece of equipment that was a little frightening in appearance, much more than its actual danger. Accidents were not common with this piece of equipment because of its closeness to the ground and its great weight. However, accidents did happen at rare intervals.

Anything as spectacular as firefighting must have its danger side. But, in telling of these accidents it is merely to bring out the fact that, never for a moment, was duty forgotten. One such accident happened in December of 1891 while Engine No. 3 was going to a fire from its firehouse on California Street, between Leaven-

worth and Hyde. On Larkin, near Sutter, the driver,
Joseph Blakely, attempted to miss a buggy that started
to pull out in front of him. There could be no reining
this fast-moving team to a stop, so he swung them
quickly over to the left side of the street where a cable
car had stopped. However, at this precise moment, the
gripman picked up his cable and started the car across
the intersection, despite the yells from the fireman who,
by this time, was going too fast to have any control over
his team, nor was there room to turn elsewhere.

Blakely pulled on the reins until his muscles bulged,
he braced his feet against the backboard, and the seat
strap pressed against his ribs. He got the fire engine
over the track but the car was too close. Engine and car
struck with a splintering crash, the force of the collision
breaking the strap that held Blakely against the seat.
Still gripping the reins he plummeted over the rumps of

*A San Francisco engine
company makes a practice
run. Note white horse in the
three-horse team.*

*—Courtesy, San Francisco
Fire Museum.*

78

79

the horses into the street. The two firemen riding on the back of the engine were hurled over the hind wheels and landed so hard onto the pavement that they were momentarily stunned. The impact pulled the horses off their feet but they began struggling wildly to free themselves. Nothing could withstand the battering ram of hooves, and in a matter of minutes the harness was broken. Struggling wildly to their feet the horses attempted to free themselves, but their collars still held fast. Leaping forward, they jerked the cable car off the track. This freed their engine, and they went dashing down the street with it.

There was no driver at the reins, but Blakely regained consciousness and, struggling to his feet, dashed after the runaways—unsteadily at first, but picking up speed as he gained strength. He began to run faster as he gathered more of his faculties, and finally he caught up

Displacing horse-drawn for motor-driven apparatus, at Engine Company 20, 2117 Filbert Street, Sept. 19, 1915.

—Courtesy, San Francisco Fire Museum.

with the team some distance down the hill. He leaped to grab the nigh horse by the bridle. The leather came apart in his hands, freeing the animal from the balance of the harness.

Wrapping the dangling parts of the reins around the horse's neck Blakely held on, but the off horse, still fastened to the engine, galloped on ahead down the hill. Finally, without much control, the one horse ran the engine into a water trough and quit, still panting with fright, but too exhausted to fight anymore. One of the other firemen caught up with Blakely and held the one horse. There was still the fire engine to think of.

The runaway engine, unattended, was making steam all over the place. There was a chance, in the collision, that the valves were damaged. This might mean an explosion of the boiler. Blakely, handing the horse's broken reins to the firemen, raced toward the steaming engine. When he reached the water trough he saw he was not far wrong. The boiler, making a low, ominous sound, was about to go. It was puffing and throbbing in a warning manner, and he knew there was no time to be lost. By now the third fireman had reached the scene. Blakely shouted directions and the horse was freed from the last remnants of the damaged harness and led away.

Blakely worked frantically and bravely to rake the coals out from the hot box under the boiler. It was not a moment too soon. Finally he stood back to take a breath, as the noise subsided, and the boiler began to cool. This was a day to be remembered by three firemen. The engine went to the repair shop and the horses went to the lay-up stables for a thorough checkup. Yes, the pump engine was the one piece of equipment that kept the public at a distance.

The cast iron boiler of the steam engine was covered with a sheet of brass or copper and sometimes nickel-plated. The smoke-stack was encircled with a handsomely rounded and beveled dome and cylinder, and the whole surface was buffed and polished, bright as a mirror. The visible working parts of the machinery were turned into decorative shapes where possible, and given a high sheen. The wheels and the body frame carried the colorful designs and striping of her predecessors. Piston pumps were the rule, although the rotary type gradually gained in favor.

Probably the next wagon in importance was the hose wagon. It was reasonably sized and carried, besides hoses, chemical equipment and a few short ladders. The hose wagon, though top-heavy with men, pulling on their rubber coats, rolled along like a well-oiled sulky. It was smooth and quiet, except for the bell, and the clopping of the lightweight team.

The ladder truck was long and gangling. It swayed and rocked with its heavy bank of clattering ladders—the tillerman high on top in the rear, with a tense hold on the wheel that governed the turning of the back wheels under the aerial ladder, his coat tails flying in the wind. Out in front of the lumbering truck, the heavy, broad-chested horses took the great weight and length of their load through traffic and around the turns. It took considerable floor space to house all this equipment.

The Victorian firehouses were, and some still are, a familiar sight in American cities. Behind the big, black doors, were housed the steam pumper, aerial ladder, alarm, telegraph, swinging harness, water tower, turret gun, rubber-lined hose, cellar pipe, life net, chemical tank, brass pole, deluge set, and an hundred other vital devices. With them were all the experience and hard-learned lessons of the firemen, and the ability of their well-trained horses. All this went to make up a complete firehouse. It sounds like a lot of upkeep, and it was, but with the routine, daily care and with the work spread around to all the men in the firehouse, it did not take a lot of time. In the first few years of trial many changes had taken place. There was even time for leisure.

On warm days the firemen sat on benches outside the firehouse. Even the horses, tied under the trees in the yard switched their tails lazily at the equally lazy flies.

The main floor was dark save for a small lamp on the watch desk and the lanterns that hung, one on each side of the hose wagon, steam engine, ladder truck and chief's carriage. The signal gongs and a wall telephone that linked the firehouse to headquarters and to every corner and alley in the city, and the automatic switching, levers and push buttons that operated the various alarms, release devices and house lights in the station, were all in a compact space against the wall toward the front of the room. By now the fire service had come a long way.

There sat the man on watch, at a tilt-top desk on which the journal lay opened and ready to take the record of the next alarm. He sat alone at the desk. The house rules kept all the other firemen upstairs or out in the yard, except when there was an alarm or fire, or when they had some station duty to perform. It was a

Matched grays and shining engine clatter along the bricked streets of the city.

—Courtesy, San Francisco Fire Museum.

82

lonely job, away from the gang for a four to six hour shift of duty. But he knew his hours of leisure would come, and someone would take his place. And the horses knew when their favorite fireman had to work, or when he was using his leisure hours at card playing.

Jerry, a hefty bay was so fond of his driver that he attempted to follow him everywhere. One day when the fireman, on his off time, was playing cards upstairs in the lounge, he heard a familiar neigh and the sound of iron shoes on wood. When he and the others got up from the card table to investigate, they were startled to see Jerry standing at the head of the stairs. When the big bay saw his favorite driver he nickered with joy, and walked into the room.

The men tried to turn Jerry around and lead him back down the stairs, but he refused to move. They tried backing him, but he wouldn't step down the first tread. Finally, they could see it was of no use. It took a block and tackle and another team to remove the big horse from the second floor. First, the large front window of the firehouse had to be removed, frame and all. It took all the men, off duty, to man the tackle, drive the team, and guide the big horse to the ground.

Even though most of the antics of the horses broke the monotony and amused the men, neither Jerry or his favorite fireman were popular around the firehouse for some time to come. But such interruptions as this helped to give the man at the desk something to muse over, as he sat looking at the shining equipment that was the pride of his house.

Nearest to the watch's desk stood the hose wagon, rich, red, flat, with glossy sides. Beside the wagon was the steamer. On the other side of the room stretched the long aerial-ladder truck, with its Big Stick lying at a slightly upward angle toward the rear, where the tip nearly touched the very back of the house. The tillerman's seat was so high his hair would mop the ceiling if he didn't bend over at the wheel.

83

Turned down boots stood waiting in pairs about the floor, rubber coats, with insides up so the sleeve holes could be found in a hurry, hung conveniently over knobby parts of the apparatus. Between the hose wagon and the ladder truck was the chief's black carriage, small, delicate. Over the dashboard hung the chief's white coat and white helmet and the driver's cap and jacket.

The yawning harness swung over the front of each kit, and the ropes from the ceiling held it up. The air in the firehouse was a blend of horse, hay and oats—oil and grease on the apparatus—the kerosene lanterns—the smell of steam machinery—saddle-soaped harness—waxed wood and polished brass.

In congested city areas two aerial-ladder trucks were usually assigned to a first alarm, not only for the possible rescue work, but also for their great value in attacking fire on the upper floors. At first the aerial ladder, so often called the Big Stick, was raised by hand cranks, so geared that two men could manage the heavy load quite well. This manual labor was shortly done away with by employing a set of cog springs packed in cylinders, which, when released, lifted the ladder in a few seconds. It could be locked in any angle and the fly extended by hand cranks. Some aerial ladders were raised by compressed air, hydraulic press, or power from a gasoline-truck motor. The Big Stick swung from window to window or floor to flooor.

At the turn of the century these trucks also carried fourteen or fifteen other ladders of assorted lengths, as well as lanterns, axes, plaster hooks, ropes, extinguishers, extra hose, nozzles and couplings, door openers, augers, rams, saws, mauls, picks, hammers, chisels, roof and wire cutters, acetylene torches, buckets, hose-repair kits, rope gun, smoke masks, rubber gloves, first aid kit, and searchlights. It is hard to think that all this equipment would be needed at a fire. Of course, many times just the basic things were used, but the rest must always be available for any emergency.

Directing water effectively from the street into a fire above the fourth floor had always been a problem. A stream thrown from the street was often useless, because its force had been spent by the time it reached a fourth floor window. A hose elevator was designed. It consisted of staging that could be raised to varying lengths up to fifty feet, and from which one or two firemen could direct hose streams into the fourth, fifth and sixth story windows.

The water tower could be fixed at heights ranging from 45 to 65 feet, and the nozzle could be controlled from the base of the tower. Water could be taken through four or six inlets, making it possible to throw a forceful stream of as much as 1200 gallons per minute. The wagons were also fitted with a deck pipe that could be operated with equal force and effect on lower floors.

But with all this equipment, it was still the thundering steam engine with the engineer poking channel coal into the hot box, and the shining stack pouring black smoke, that the public remembered best. It is remarkable to consider the start of the department with one small piece of equipment, pulled by the men themselves, to this well equipped, well trained, well organized service. Necessity invariably demands, suggests, and invents what is needed for efficiency.

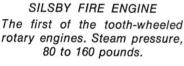

SILSBY FIRE ENGINE
The first of the tooth-wheeled
rotary engines. Steam pressure,
80 to 160 pounds.

85

The motor displaces the horse at the Washington Street firehouse, September 19, 1915.

—Courtesy, San Francisco Fire Museum.

The Pension Plan

THE COLORFUL days of San Francisco's Fire Department which involved the fire-horse will live in the memory of families whose fathers and grandfathers helped to build its reputation. Many oldsters, today, can sit back and tell and retell the stories they remember of seeing those famous horses at work, their visits to the firehouse, their listening to the firemen tell about the favorite horses. Only in the hidden, forgotten and perhaps dusty files of the newspaper are the factual stories of excitement, acts of heroism, tales of devotion to duty, and the inevitable death and disaster that also were a part of this era.

Many hours of digging through these files, of talking to retired firemen, searching through scrapbooks, has resulted in producing the pages of this book. And, yet, there is little picture of disaster and more of the happy ending for this fabulous history.

When one thinks of the geography of San Francisco, its great hills, with their tremendously steep grades, then one realizes that the use of horses to draw the fire equipment was something of an undertaking. It becomes clear why this city could easily boast of the most picturesque fire department in the country. I doubt that any other city can show steeper grades. Even today pedestrians sometimes back up the sidewalks of these steep streets, so it can be imagined that for a team to pull any kind of wagon up one of these grades would be next to impossible. However, much of this was handled by routing along cross streets in order to traverse these grades. It was, indeed, an age of specialization. It combined ingenuity, engineering and plain old "horse sense."

Horses and men had to be a special type. The men, to live a life of being wet, smudged by smoke and soot; to face danger of falling walls, and the possibility of being trapped by heavy timbers. And yet, neither horse nor man ever flinched from duty. Gallant deeds were the part of both horses and men—never failing to accept the situation, and sometimes giving their lives in meeting an emergency while badly injured. Such stories fill many pages of records of the department's history and I have tried to bring forth the most interesting ones in this book.

But there is no explanation of the courage and stamina that urged these living beings to expose themselves to danger. To ask a fireman why, would only bring the answer that it was a duty to be done. Yet, the fireman never thought of giving up. There was an excitement and a thrill that even the men themselves couldn't explain.

For the horses there couldn't have been this sort of reasoning—only the urge to do the duty they had been trained for. For example: Teddy Roosevelt, a powerful bay gelding, lived to the age of seventeen years, fifteen of these in the same firehouse and at the same post on the wagon. He was one of the department's finest, and never lost a day's work, or threw a shoe during his long service. And if the horses could have added their stories of violence and disaster caused by fire, it might have been told by a horse named Barney, who had the same driver for fourteen years. If one tried to tell all the tales in Barney's life they would almost fill a book.

Barney belonged to Engine House No. 17, and his story would have gone like this: According to his driver, Barney saw a wall bulge, forced out by a collection of gases. He saw it fall, burying a water tower, which, in turn, engulfed horses, men and a wagon. He saw two fire engines, answering a three alarm fire, meet head on, and the pole of one buried in the side of a luckless bay horse. All these things upset him, of course, but never once did he try to run away or disobey a command, even in the face of such possible accidents.

But these dreadful disasters were few and far between, and accepted as part of the life of the department. Indeed, looking out toward the calm waters of the bay it was hard to believe that, many times, Barney watched tongues of flame changing the skyline of the city.

When Barney finally ended his days in the peaceful pastures of Martinez, it was difficult to picture the hills around the Golden Gate, rising serene and undisturbed, ever being disfigured by billowing smoke. But changes come, whether by disaster, demand or time.

Even though the horses went in for periodic check-ups, it wasn't unusual for a good horse to spend from fourteen to sixteen years in the service. A completely sound animal was a must in any firehouse, and these check-ups were a form of insurance, and accrual age had little to do with the length of service.

Even when a firehorse began to lose his speed, he wasn't discarded. His loyalty was never forgotten by the department, and they did everything to keep him in the service that was such a part of his life. When it was decided that a horse must be relinquished, he was first transferred to outlying districts, where alarms were less frequent. Bohockey Hop was one of these.

He was a long, rangy bay from Engine No. 9. He was also proof that firehorses reason and think for themselves. He learned that by kicking the iron post of his stall he could release the "let-go" chain across the front of his stall. He liked to wander about, and many times was found grazing on the lawn across the street. When he slowed down, he was sold to a sausage company, and began pulling a delivery wagon.

One day, passing a station, the gong sounded. At the sight of the fire engines, he leaped forward to go with them. He went all the way to the fire, scattering sausages along the street. When the driver finally caught up with him at the fire, there was Bohockey Hop standing at attention.

In the first days of the department, when at last a horse was not even valuable in a minor district, it was to the auction he went. These horses were not readily salable because of their habit of answering fire alarms, so this fact brought their price down. And because of their low price, they were often bought by those who needed a strong animal to do menial work. Many times they were so degraded as to be seen pulling a rag picker's wagon. It was a double hardship upon the horses, when they were used to good bedding and excellent

Displacing horse-drawn for first motor-driven fire truck, Van Ness Avenue. Photo taken September 17, 1912.
—Courtesy, San Francisco Fire Museum.

90

feed, daily grooming and special care for the feet. It was indeed a sad ending for a noble creature.

From the well run stables, and the careful, routine attention, the auction block was a long step for them to take. But the public does not forget service. It only needs to be reminded of the prestige the horses gave to the department.

Little G, after an injury going to a fire, was condemned to the auction block. Her injury was caused by going through a trap door at a fire, and when the veterinarian shook his head at further use to the service, she was put up for sale. Here the power of the press was evident, when the newspaper announced the sale, with an article about the faithful little mare's loyalty to the city. And it ended with the question of what was to become of her. When the paper received some letters in response to the article, then a series appeared about

The "new look" in fire engines, San Francisco Fire Department, a dozen years into the 20th Century.

—Courtesy, San Francisco Fire Museum.

other horses. The public began to take notice, and read the articles eagerly.

The future plight of Little G became a popular dinner topic, and the public began to rouse. Everyone is familiar with the expression "like an old firehorse." The public, taking this expression literally, came forward to start a fund for Little G. Then someone suggested a pension, and such a retirement for the firehorses became a real issue. But it was largely due to the efforts of veterinary surgeon William F. Eagen, and Matthew McCurrie of the S.P.C.A. that the famous firehorses won a secure retirement pension, instead of drudgery and death after years of faithful service.

The little mare was never sold. The public worked, guided by Dr. Eagen, until a pension plan was well established for all firehorses. Most of them were sent to a large pasture in Martinez, across the bay, to end their days peacefully cropping grass, far from the sound of the bells that made them jump to duty. A few went to do light work in Golden Gate Park, but they were well cared for. And, if they did get excited when they heard a fire bell, they were forgiven and admired for their long lasting faithfulness.

It was an era that took a great deal to establish. But it did much to further the art of firefighting. Many innovations became operative, and proved that "necessity is the mother of invention." Because the problems presented by horse drawn apparatus caused much revision, it lessened those of the motorized era when it came into being. Even the parades were made more colorful by the shining, red wagons, and the well groomed horses and their polished harness. No parade was ever complete without them.

Here and there a story can be pinpointed about a specific horse. One called Mike had such a place, because he was the last firehorse to ever be purchased by the department.

Mike was a large black, with a white forehead and white fetlocks. In 1919 he was turned over to Golden

Gate Park for light work. In 1934 he was sent to pasture in Martinez, where he died, August 29, 1934. He was twenty-seven years old. Here, too, coincidence plays a part. The last horse purchased was also the last horse to die. Changes were surely taking place.

In August of 1921, San Francisco Engine Company No. 6 responded to the last fire in which horses were used. An hour and fifteen minutes later, or after this fire, the company was mechanized. There was a trace of tears in the eyes of the men as they watched the horses led down the street toward the lay-up stables. The pounding of iron hooves on pavement, rushing to a fire, would never be heard again. The last firehorses left the department stables on December 31, 1921, when the stables were officially closed.

The change came as a surprise and a disappointment to the firemen and the citizens. Few people, today, can remember hearing the fire warning, how they counted the blasts to determine the direction of the fire, and then ran to the door to watch the dashing horses and the red wagons racing down the street. Never again would there be disturbances at night as some mischievous horse figured a way to get an extra portion of grain. Never again would there sound the friendly whinnies along the stalls as a beloved driver was recognized. Their work was done. The firehorse's future would only be dawn and twilight, with pasture-filled days.

The whole firehouse was now quiet, with the silence of motors waiting for fire calls. Cold, inanimate things of steel and iron they were, that only warmed when the motor was started. Part of the thrill was gone, and only the excitement of an actual fire was left to wait for. Silk handkerchiefs were discarded because there were no satiny, warm coats left to inspect. Instead, a shiny red motor—that only required an oiled dustcloth.

As the motorized units began to creep into the fire fighting world the horses gradually diminished. The minor districts were the last to motorize. Visitors to the firehouses were fewer, except for those curious about

93

the motors. But you can't feed a carrot to a motor. Those days have long passed and yet, today, the fire apparatus moves no faster than in the old days, because of the present heavy flow of traffic.

But the horse's accomplishment can never be forgotten. They have served man wherever and whenever needed since their discovery as beasts of burden, transportation and companionship. And again, in reminiscing, we must not forget that Pennsylvania Company responded, with its three black horses, to the first fire. As San Francisco Company No. 6, it responded to the last fire with horses—again three black ones. And so, with the ending of this book one is reminded that the horse gave much more than service. No other horse in any other capacity can make this claim. For this noble animal—the San Francisco Firehorse—there never was retirement.